THE
BLOB

BY HAYLEY LEE

ILLUSTRATIONS BY
SCOTT A. SCHEIDLY

Harcourt Brace & Company

Orlando Atlanta Austin Boston San Francisco Chicago Dallas New York Toronto London

I got my sled and went
up the hill. The hill was
slick, but I didn't slip.

Then I saw it! It was a
blue slab, a blue glob! It
was the BIG BLUE BLOB!

"Click, click! Blip, blip!"
said the blob.
"HELP!" I said. I jumped
flat on my sled and fled!

4

Down I slid. Down slid the big blue blob! We were flying over a cliff! Flip, flop! Flip, flop! PLOP! PLOP!

There I was with the big
blue blob. The blob
looked at me and said,
"Glug, glug. Glug, glug."

Then my mom said, "Get up! Look at the clock!"
"WHAT?" I said.

I was in bed!

Boy, was I glad!